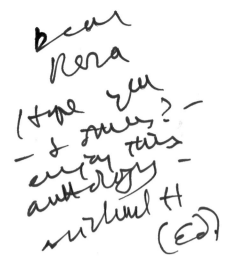

The **POM!** (Poetry **O**lympics **M**arathon) Anthology
Edited by Michael Horovitz
New Departures #32

Published in 2001 by New Departures,
PO Box 9819, London W11 2GQ

www.connectotel.com/PoetryOlympics

Designed by Satpaul Bhamra
with Michael Horovitz and David Russell

A CIP catalogue record for this book
is available from the British Library.

ISBN 0 902689 21 5

Poetry Olympics Marathon

Allen Ginsberg and Paul McCartney performing Allen's 'Ballad of the Skeletons'
at the Royal Albert Hall on 16 October 1995, by Linda McCartney

Gregory Corso and Anselm Hollo at 'Live New Departures' in the Café des Artistes, Chelsea
in 1962, by the late lamented Maurice Hatton

Beryl Bainbridge receiving her Damehood from Queen Elizabeth II at Buckingham Palace, by Brendan King; the crown and annotated flag were subsequently drawn onto it by Beryl, commemorating the wondrous coincidence that she was made an official Dame of the British Empire on 21 November 2000 – her 66th birthday!

Michael Horovitz, Fran Landesman and Patience Agbabi at the press launch of the POP! (Poetry Olympics Party) festival at the Royal Festival Hall in Spring 2000, by Ifigenija Simonovic

TORCH SONGS
for a truly Brave New World

Bizarrely, it was Margaret Thatcher who gave birth to the Poetry Olympics. In the autumn of 1980 she did her utmost to boycott the participation of British athletes in the Moscow Olympics – a tad unsporting of the boss cow methought. Largely on account of the monetarist/Little Englandist fangs of Maggie's Farm and Philip Larkin's toadies, the jazz, beat and protest poetry flowerings of the Sixties were being trashed in favour of the yuppie careerist nillennium.

The result was that official verse-making in Britain sank back into the post-war WASPish game reserve which excluded so many who were made to feel that poetry was not for them. Mindful that the Olympics originally featured celebrations of all the arts, our New Departures team launched the first Poetry Olympics from Westminster Abbey for the pursuit of excellence and Healing of the Nations.

It's my hope that the hymn book of our 21st birthday party you're looking at, with work by each writer involved in relaying the first Poetry Olympics Marathon, will provide strength, solace, entertainment and inspiration. For my money, every text here projects the diversity and vitality of the essential body poetic that hands on the baton of artistic commitment which, in the words of imagination's patron saint William Blake, *". . . present, past & future sees"*.

As well as a nucleus of living torchbearers, relish in this cornucopia poems by a few celestially absented friends of the sacred flame: Gregory Corso, Allen Ginsberg and Frances Horovitz, alongside Jill Neville representing the salt and wizardry of Oz (and proving that *P-O-M* doesn't mean our range confines itself to poor old mother England's brood) – and Anselm Hollo, the bardic Finn who was in at the beginnings of New Departures forty years ago, now lost by Albion to the Jack Kerouac School of Disembodied Poetics in Boulder, Colorado.

✦

The generous contributions of Paul McCartney and Hank Wangford will doubtless irritate the ignorant hirelings who greeted Paul's first volume of *Poems and Lyrics 1965–1999* with such a pompous chorus of disapproval in the would-be intellectual press – but that's not why they're here. Both are authentic poets, with their music and without it: the word *"lyric"*, remember, stems from *"poetry sung to lyre accompaniment"*.

Those Blue Meanie reviewers also need reminding of Dr Johnson's view that *"no man was ever writ down but by himself"*. Several of them dismissed Macca's collection of some 150 texts out of hand without so much as one brief quotation. The Observer's pseudo-critic was fairly typical in repetitiously sneering at the author of 'Eleanor Rigby', 'Penny Lane' and 'When I'm 64' for not *only* alleged "lack of technical control over language", but *also* "linguistic ineptitude". . . Indulging this sort of unsubstantiated abuse whilst not even mentioning the last twenty pages devoted to the lyrist's late wife and muse, Linda McCartney – like them or not – is as hypercritically crap as a piece supposedly engaging with Ted Hughes's complete poetry would be if it failed even to allude to his poems for Sylvia Plath.

Form your own impression, dear reader, by sampling the work itself – for example, by – er, observing, how in 'Meditate' (pages 56–57), McCartney outstares the random reflections that crowd the surface of the well of self until, having described their own arc, they eventually kiss the joy where it flies.

✦

I'm writing this in the week the Presidents of America and Britain have explicitly Declared War on the selfsame planet they've been ravaging and savaging with slightly less self-advertisement ever since each of them took office. I hope I speak for all of the New Departures/Poetry Olympics troubadours in imploring world leaders to temper and overcome their reflex kneejerk headline-grabbing rabble-rousing eye-for-an-eye reactions to the 11th September '01 Fall of Wall Street, and Agony of the Pentagon, with historical perspectives and creative intelligence.

Let them meditate on the self-destructive fate of so many would-be almighty triumphalist power-monoliths, from the Tower of Babel to the Greenwich Dome. Have they learned nothing from Nato's disastrous series of military incursions over the Balkans, whose most recent bomb-happy escapade only multiplied *every*one's troubles in spades?

If it took 25,000 astronomically expensive bombing raids to "take out" no more than thirteen Serbian tanks, whilst inflicting aeons of murderous and ecological "collateral damage", why would the heaviest arms resources of the [Western] world dismantle unspecified numbers of unidentified terrorists in unknown parts of Afghanistan, rather than disrupt and massacre ever more innumerable innocents – and pollute ever more of the lands, water and air *all* humans are given to use and nurture?

✦

Just *try*
to THINK,
Cruise-Aider Blair
and your toxic Texan confrère George Bush, over there
in silly-con missile Valhalla,
please, think
(stop fiddling with oilmen while forests burn),
on T S Eliot's prediction
of the ultimate
doomed waste land
your uncontrollably spiralling military glands
could grind all ships of state towards

– upon which

". . . the dead tree gives no shelter, the cricket no relief,
And the dry stone no sound of water. Only
There is shadow under this red rock,
(Come in under the shadow of this red rock),
And I will show you something different from either
Your shadow at morning striding behind you
Or your shadow at evening rising to meet you;
I will show you fear in a handful of dust . . ."

Put on your red dress, baby,
let me button up my blue jeans.
You revitalise me daily,
you're the life-blood running through my veins.

You're the setting sun in my clear blue sky
and in my midnight-blue you're the harvest moon.
Sometimes we argue and I don't know why,
you're Mars and I'm Neptune.

You accuse me of quenching your fire:
I accuse you of blocking my flow
but you're the ruby to my sapphire,
you're the bright red cherry to my blue-black sloe.

You're the red rag to my raging bull.
You always see red when I sing the blues.
You're the ladybird tracing the ridge of my clavicle.
You're the lipstick on my collar, I'm your blue suede shoes.

You're the redbreast on my blue velvet.
I'm the aerogramme in your postbox.
You're my ruby slippers, you're my red carpet.
I'm the poet but baby, you're my thought-fox.

You're the red in enamoured, you're wicked.
You're Scarlett O'Hara, I'm Betty Blue.
I'm the blue pill in *The Matrix* and you're the red.
You're my red phone bill, overdue.

You've got more kick than red rum,
you're red raw, red-handed, red-hot.
I metamorphose into blue nun.
You're love-lies-bleeding, I'm forget-me-not.

You say we were a mismatched couple
but I'm reminiscing too.
I remember how we made the colour purple
and my eyes are red from missing you.

THE CHANGE

I remember everything vividly that Sunday
by its absence. It was the day that God,
like Father Christmas and the tooth fairy,
no longer existed. The church smelt musty
and I noticed Mrs Leadbetter's glass eye.
I remember lip synching the Lord's Prayer

and Amen after father murmured grace
for Sunday dinner. At the head of the table
sat a leg of lamb, more like a sacrifice
than a roast. Our golden Labrador, Petra,
sloped off into the sitting room, and hid.

Father carved while mother served raw carrots,
puréed swede and something resembling cabbage.
I can still taste it in the back of my throat.
The only sound was stainless steel on china

till I realised the potatoes were missing
and said it, and my mother turned, a blur
of plate spinning across the room and breaking.

My father said "She's going through The Change".
I stared into the kitchen floor and wondered

what, in God's name, she was changing into.

THE STING

At twelve I learnt about The Fall,
had rough-cut daydreams based on original sin,
nightmares about the swarm of thin-
lipped, foul-mouthed, crab apple-
masticating girls who'd chase me full
throttle: me, slipping on wet leaves, a heroine
in a black-and-white cliché; them, buzzing on nicotine
and the sap of French kisses. I hated big school
but even more, I hated the lurid shame
of surrender, the yellow miniskirt
my mother wore the day that that man
drove my dad's car to collect me. She called my name
softly, more seductive than an advert.
I heard the drone of the engine, turned and ran.

ON POETRY
AND DR JOHNSON

I know little about poetry, possibly because at school I was given to understand it was a separate discipline from that of prose. To this day I know by heart *The Slave's Dream*, *The Lady of Shalott*, *"A highwayman came riding . . ."*, and *"They told me, Heraclitus, they told me you were dead . . ."* In my head – which, although dependent upon my heart, is further away from it – I still hold bits of T S Eliot, Auden and Louis MacNeice, most especially that poem by the latter which begins, *"The sunlight on the garden/ Hardens and grows cold . . ."*

Beyond these few examples, all learnt in childhood, I remain ignorant, and yet without them I would find it difficult to write prose, for I rely on the sound and rhythm of words when endeavouring to construct a sentence. To try to achieve this I say aloud everything I intend to write down, and not until it seems to me that the *"tum-te-tums"* of what I am reciting have the right sound, do I commit the words to paper.

For instance, when composing a paragraph to do with a post mortem of Dr Samuel Johnson in 1784, I originally wrote –

"Reaching Windmill Street the cart was pulled into the yard of William Hunter's School of Anatomy. The carpet was carried to the top floor and laid on a dissecting table . . . . In the corner of the room, a dog, half-flayed, hung from a hook in the ceiling. Grey heavens touched the skylight."

This was eventually changed to –

> ". . . *Arriving in* Windmill Street the cart *trundled* into the
> yard, etc . . . In the corner of the *cosy* room, a dog, half-
> flayed, hung from a hook in the ceiling; *above, the* grey heavens
> *nudged* the skylight."

✦

*[There follow two excerpts from Beryl's novel, 'According to Queeney'
(Little, Brown, 2001), which presents an account of Dr Johnson's long and
crucial relationship with the vivacious Mrs Hester Thrale, recounted by her
hitherto overlooked oldest daughter – Ed.]*

For the remainder of the day Baretti kept to the school-room.
Nor did he join the guests at dinner, and instead requested food be
brought to his chamber, for which relief Mrs Thrale gave heartfelt
thanks. It enabled her to pay proper attention to the discussion of a
new work undertaken by Johnson, for which a committee of the most
reputable booksellers in London were proposing to pay him two
hundred pounds. The publication would consist of accounts of the
lives of the English poets and criticism of their verse; Sam was
honeyed enough to declare, in the presence of Dr Burney, who had
been persuaded to stop the night, that he would appreciate her help.
His exact words were, "Your judgement, my dear, is of value, for you
are not burdened by excessive scholarship and your perception
is fresh."

Mrs Thrale immediately insisted on the inclusion of Milton and
Gray, the one, in parts a favourite of them both, the other, in her
opinion, a poet vastly overrated, *'The Prospect of Eton College'*, in
particular, suggesting nothing which every beholder was not capable
of thinking or feeling for themselves. "Gray's supplication to Father
Thames", she elaborated, "to divulge who drove the hoop or tossed
the ball, is useless and puerile."

"Well said, Madam," cried Johnson and patted her fondly on the
head. Some weeks before, troubled with an infestation of the scalp,
she had left off wearing her wig. Both he and Henry had applauded
the change in her appearance and gone so far as to claim they saw
moonbeams dancing in her hair.

✦

Johnson was walking along Fleet Street, his gaze directed towards the ground, when his eye chanced upon the muscular tail of a rat protruding from a litter of old newspapers blown against the doorway of a pie shop. He was thinking that particular moment of Dryden, of whom he had written, *The power that predominated in his intellectual operations was rather strong reason than quick sensibility*, a sentence he had reworked several times, for it seemed to him that he was dissecting himself rather than his subject. Had not Dryden been in possession of a mind stored with principles and observations? Were not his performances always hasty, either excited by some external occasion, or extorted by domestic necessity? Did he not compose without consideration and publish without correction? What his mind could supply at call, or gather in one excursion was all he sought, for he had no love of labour . . .

Distracted, he stopped to observe the emergence of the rodent. Out it came, snout sniffing the air, forepaws raised. It saw, or sensed, him – and was gone in an instant.

Almost at once he was hailed by James Boswell, yesterday returned from Scotland and on his way to Bolt Court hoping to find him at home. Puce with excitement, Boswell cried out, "Sir, I am happy to see you," and wrung his hand.

When they had tripped through the politenesses, Johnson said, "The sight of an animal going about its business, seeking its food, foraging for its young – what a strange pleasure it affords us."

"True, true," Boswell affirmed, though he could see nothing but birds strutting the gutter.

"There is only one mendacious being in the world", continued Johnson, "and that is man. Every other is virtuous and sincere."

"True, true," repeated Boswell, and begged to be allowed to walk with him, for, he said, he had now read a great proportion of the manuscript of *Critical Observations on the Poets*, and longed to have talk of it. Johnson replied that he was just now in a reflective mood, but, if it would please him, he would be welcome that evening at Bolt Court.

As they parted, he said, "The main reason we take so much pleasure in looking at the lower animals is because we like to see our own nature in a simplified form." This observation appeared to him so apt that he began to chuckle at his perspicacity, an outburst that got the better of him and developed into full-throated laughter, upon which the pigeons rose in a disordered flock and swirled about his head.

ORDINARY MAWNING

it wasn't dat de day did start out bad
or dat no early mawning dream
did swing mi foot
aff de wrong side of de bed

it wasn't dat de cold floor
mek me sneeze
an mi nose start run wid misery
wasn't a hangover headache
mawning
or a worry rising mawning

de sun did shine same way
an a cool breeze
jus a brush een aff de sea
an de mawning news
was jus de same as ever
two shot dead
truck lick one
Israel still a bruk up
Palestine

no
it wasn't de day dat start out bad
wasn't even pre m t
or post m t
was jus anadda ordinary get up
get de children ready fi school
mawning
anadda wanda what to cook fah dinna dis evening
mawning
anadda wish me never did breed but Lawd
mi love dem mawning
jus anadda wanda if ah should a
tek up back wid dis man it would a
ease de situation mawning

no
it wasn't no duppy frighten mi
mek mi jump outa mi sleep
eena bad mood
nor no neighbour bring first quarrel
to mi door
wasn't de price rise pon bus fare
an milk an sugar

was jus anadda
same way mawning
anadda clean up de mess
after dem lef mawning
a perfectly ordinary
mawning of a perfectly
ordinary day
trying to fine a way
out

so it did hard fi understand
why de ordinary sight of
mi own frock
heng up pon line
wid some clothespin
should a stop me from do nutten
but jus
bawl

REPATRIATION

I seek
repatriation
into love

for love created I
among the cool ferns
on a river's morning

and Riva Mumma's hair
was casting glances of the sun
like mirrors on the rock

love danced with I
wrapped in hot tambric leaves
sprayed with ginger lilies
picking kisses
like roseapples

sweet sticky starapple days
melted
into chocolate evenings

and night
would fold its petals round I
like a lover
home to rest

for love
created I
among the cool ferns
on a river's
morning

DREAMER

roun a rocky corner
by de sea
seat up
pon a drif wood
yuh can fine she
gazin cross de water
a stick
eena her han
tryin to trace
a future
in de san

ESSENTIAL CUTS

D'you like my fabby face lift?
The swelling's almost down,
The stitches hardly hurt at all
– Unless I smile or frown.

The nose is awfully cute, I think;
It's perfect now, no doubt.
The only tricky bit, I find,
Is breathing in . . . and out.

My boobs are still quite painful,
But they'll settle down with wear;
A bargain – buy one, get one free
– For an *almost* matching pair.

I'm bankrupt and can't seem to move
As freely as I should,
But what's a little suffering
When it comes to looking good?

Girls who are A-cups
Just long to be Ds.
They dream of low necklines
That plunge to their knees.

They'd kill for real cleavage
Their thoughts are obsessed
With men trampolining
For joy on their chests.

Girls with big bosoms
Are sick of their size
And long for a man who'll
Look into their eyes.

CLAIRE CALMAN

17

THE WHOLE MESS . . . ALMOST

I ran up six flights of stairs
to my small furnished room
opened the window
and began throwing out
those things most important in life

First to go, Truth, squealing like a fink:
"Don't! I'll tell awful things about you!"
"Oh yeah? Well, I've nothing to hide . . . OUT!"
Then went God, glowering & whimpering in amazement:
"It's not my fault! I'm not the cause of it all!" "OUT!"
Then Love, cooing bribes: "You'll never know impotency!
All the girls on *Vogue* covers, all yours!"
I pushed her gushy ass out screaming:
"You always end up a bummer!"
I picked up Faith Hope Charity
all three clinging together:
"Without us you'll surely die!"
"With you I'm going nuts! Goodbye!"

Then Beauty . . . ah, Beauty —
As I led her to the window
I told her: "You I loved best in life
. . . but you're a killer; Beauty kills!"
Not really meaning to drop her
I immediately ran downstairs
getting there just in time to catch her
"You saved me!" she cried
I put her down and told her: "Move on."

Ran back up those six flights
went to the money
there was no money to throw out.
The only thing left in the room was Death
hiding beneath the kitchen sink:
"I'm not real!" It droned
"I'm just a rumour spread by life . . ."
Laughing I threw it out, kitchen sink and all
and suddenly realized Humour
was all that was left —
All I could do with Humour was laugh, saying:
"Out the window with the window!"

GREGORY CORSO

PORTLAND COLISEUM

A brown piano in diamond
    white spotlight
Leviathan auditorium
    iron rib wired
    hanging organs, vox
        black battery
A single whistling sound of
    ten thousand children's
        larynxes asinging
        pierce the ears
    and flowing up the belly
    bliss the moment arrived

Apparition, four brown English
    jacket christhair boys
Goofed Ringo battling bright
        white drums
Silent George hair patient
        Soul horse

Short black-skulled Paul
    with thin guitar
Lennon the Captain, his mouth
    a triangular smile,
all jump together to End
    some tearful memory song
        ancient two years,

    The million children
    the thousand worlds
bounce in their seats, bash
        each other's sides, press
        legs together nervous
Scream again & claphand
      become one Animal
      in the New World Auditorium
   – hands waving myriad
      snakes of thought
      screech beyond hearing

while a line of police with
      folded arms stands
Sentry to contain the red
      sweatered ecstasy
    that rises upward to the
        wired roof.

August 27, 1965

GRANDAD'S GLASSES

Grandad's going underground tomorrow
in a mahogany box,
it was his favourite timber;
we've made the requiem arrangements
and we'll even be able to find a home
for grandad's socks and pajamas,
but when somebody passes away
there's always a problem or two:
how we gonna break it to grandad's doggie,
and what we gonna do about grandad's glasses?
What we gonna do about grandad's glasses?
He didn't like to see things wasted.
What we gonna do about grandad's glasses?
He didn't like to see things thrown away,
maybe somebody could use the frame
but it's always a shame to break a pair up;
a bus pass you can just tear up,

but you can't just tear up your grandad's glasses.
At least grandma had the sense to leave him
before he finished breathing,
you need a little joke at times like these
and grandad would have had us all having a knees up
but, what we gonna do about
grandad's glasses?

They won't be going underground with grandad,
he didn't believe in telly after death.
Opportunity no longer knocks for grandad,
he was running for the bus,
when he ran right out of breath,
and just to add one final twist
a postcard came for him this morning,
they only mis-spelt his name slightly
otherwise they put it so politely
Dear Sir or Madam
Your new spectacles
are ready for collection.
What we gonna do about grandad's glasses?
I don't mean the ones he kept his teeth in.
What we gonna do about grandad's glasses?
The ones he won't be going underneath in.
It isn't easy to realise,
that grandad's eyes are closed forever.
Now I know what a farce is,
now I know what a farce is
what we gonna do about grandad?
What we gonna do about that grand
old daddy,
and what we gonna do about grandad's
empty glasses?

Hermes Psychopompus leads Eurydice to Orpheus
(Attic bas-relief in Villa Albani, Rome)

EURYDICE AND ORPHEUS

in their own words

EURYDICE:

Dog calmed
river crossed –
the gods had made it so clear
look back and she's lost.
So, dog calmed, river crossed
why did he turn back?
Was it a chance overshoulder glance,
an absent-minded oversight
that sent him back to Hades,
or was it him checking
to see that I was still there
and then knowing
in that moment of knowing
that I was
but I wouldn't be,
or was it an upbraiding glare –
petulance at my following him,
an impulsive reprimand
for which he would reprimand himself
for the rest of his days
or was it that he just went nuts?

Or was it a celebratory sharing,
his foot upon the threshold
he turns . . .
"Eurydice, look – we're there . . ."
And then only he is there.
The overenthusiastic folly.
The premature judgement.

The complacent Greek.
What was his mistake?
The mistake is yours.
You look only at the possible errors of the man.
With the woman lies the solution.

JOHN HEGLEY

Yes, it happened at the very threshold.
But he turned because . . .
because I called him.
And why?
Because I wanted to look at him once more.
But only once.

ORPHEUS:

It wasn't an inadvertent glance, no.
And I wasn't annoyed at her following me.
So I didn't look back in anger.
And I didn't need to check
she was with me, I knew she was there alright.
So why did I do it?
It was something one head of the dog said.
"Isn't she better off in your head,
dead?
Have a think.
It's a long way to Hades."
And so I thought, is my sense of loss more sensual
than any other sensation;
if I lose this loss, do I actually gain by *having* her?
And I thought, Yes I *do* want her.
I do not want to want for her . . .
On the way back to the light
I considered the choice
And the voice inside me said
live without the lack.
Have your heart unbroke.
And then she spoke.
She said, "I've missed you so much
I'm so fond of you
You're beautiful."
And I turned around
and she was talking to the dog.

EARLY DEALINGS WITH OUR DAUGHTER

That morning
she is a month old,
I hold onto her littleness
and ask her "where are your teeth?
Where are they, where are your teeth?"
It may seem to be a daft question
but then so is any question to someone her age.
Anyway, that afternoon
we are visited by friends
and when they have gone I am told
"Imelda says her teeth are coming through."
"Really," I reply
"I was asking her about her teeth only this morning."

ON PAPER

She's sat with me here at the table
she isn't yet able to speak
she's throttling her bottle
she's only a month and a week.
I mixed her milk yesterday evening
to make up her milk from the breast
it's twenty past three in the morning
she's wearing her sleep suit and vest.
I'm writing this poem one handed
the other is feeding the muse
she's just had a wee bit of winding
and over my poem she spews.

JOHN HEGLEY

POMOLOGY

An apple a day
is 365 apples.
A poem a day
is 365 poems.
Most years.
Any doctor will tell you
it is easier to eat an apple
than to make a poem.
It is also easier
to eat a poem
than to make an apple
but only
just. But here
is what you do
to keep the doctor
out of it: publish a poem
on your appletree.
Have an apple
in your next book.

THE REFLECTION
ANSWERS NARCISSUS

I held on – couldn't help myself –
to the idea,
            just the idea,
      of love.

I gripped like a monkey
to the bottom,
            just the bottom,
      of a tree.

And all I could see, high amongst the echoing leaves,
was your face –
            like a star dribbling into stars –
      mouthing one word:

            "Enough."

THE RETURN OF ORPHEUS AND EURYDICE

i Orpheus Triumphant

We have been locked beneath the earth, walking
up a dizzy spiral, chasing the scent
of light. I dare not look back, so singing
keeps me sane, keeps me focused on the rent

earth ahead, the glory-wound of crazed stones.
Memory is a broken mosaic,
water running through a bird's hollow bones,
colour, thought and style locked in euphoric

movements, like fine clothing draped on bodies
that understand light and chime in the breeze.
No need to tell me where my dark god is.
He is just song. He is Eurydice's.

I see the sunlight's deepest perch ahead,
a bleached rock in an apple-blossom bed.

From beneath the green, we came wrapped
in darkness, spattered with jewels

like a starling's wing flickering
in death. Yet we were alive and,

against all expectation, whole –
breathing the warm air on a hill

nibbled down to felt by rabbits.
On tenterhooks we lay warming

our bones, stretched out naked to the
sudden, overpowering sun.

Soon the birds and animals came,
lured by the promise of music,

of Orpheus's haunting voice.
They dressed us in their hand-me-downs,

used us as looms, as mannequins:
wool and feathers into the weft,

cast-off snake skin into the warp.
Then Orpheus sang. The world stopped.

The sun bled silently through clouds
and leaves. I only danced, ecstatic

in my finery, a goddess
out of the green, all life renewed.

ADAM HOROVITZ

Under the crumpled lilac trees,
beneath seed beds of galaxies,
in the heat of a tulip sun,
I weave my fragile little words.

I've sewn the details of my creed
into a dog-toothed net of tweed –
a fine suit to hide meaning in
The truth is safest as a code.

Under the blackthorn and its sloes,
beneath the dogged scent of rose,
beside a crooked rivulet,
I bind my love to me with clothes.

ADAM HOROVITZ

Orpheus charms the King of Hades with his music in order to return his bride, Eurydice, to life on Earth.

this Eurydice made it –
fragmented, bloody
an unattended birth
forced out between rocks
in a barren field

the light sears

where are the flowers
the song's echo
in the season of spring?

only the voices of others
lamenting also
the shadow of Orpheus
stretching always
        over the hill
                over the hill

Frances Horovitz

Reminder

London's fair
city spring –
passed –
        unnoticed
till bare treetops
        scraped the
                bus
                roof

MH

BLANK O' CLOCK BLUES

    . . . 25 past 11
or 5 to 5??? –

makes little diff if
you're only half a - live

– is this jazz
or is it jive?

i dunno – guess
i gotta go scive

. . . someday I'll know
guess that day'll come

when I'm good an' dead
when I'm *off* the bum

– when I'm *really* gone
sounds like this
'll be my swan-song

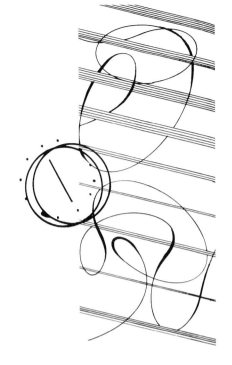

      . . . woke up this mornin'
      blues walkin' roun' my bed

      – woke up *again*   this *eve*nin'
      – still way outa' my head . . .

      when I wake (will i wake?)
      tomorrow mornin'

      – will I be   alive
                   or dead?

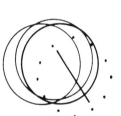

– talk 'n singin' the blues
like Langston Hughes

– adoptin' that tone
– cheery preach 'n moan

– brush aside pain

like a trickle o' rain

– that cries a stain
'cross your window pane

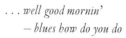

   . . . *well good mornin'*
    – blues how do you do

  well good morning – *mid*night
   – blues I wish I knew

  – when O when O when
   [*how long*] Blues :

  will i ever
     be through
       with you

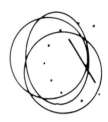

– sing it
    low as it comes
an' high when it goes

in front a' their eyes
gettin' higher
     than highs

an' deeper than spaces
behind our eyes

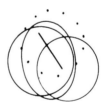

– inside our minds
when we let up the blinds

see it all without fear
– sing it out to each ear

   ". . . *Poetry – glues your soul together*
   Poetry – wears dynamite shoes
   Poetry – the spittle on the mirror
   Poetry – wears nothing but the blues . . ."

  . . . 25 past 11?
i thot it was night

MICHAEL HOROVITZ

but i couldn' git me
a bite to sleep

so i kep' right on writin'
an' writhin'
          an' ridin' –

a- zoomin' thru clouds like a ZAPoline
– jumpin' the stars on ma trampoline

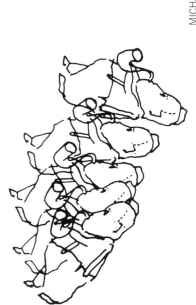

of blank-time blues that cain't be seen
– turnin' grey
              to sunshine
    an' old
         to green

      . . . if you're drivin'
make sure
         you have
             a car –

or you'll find yo'self   wonderin'
jes' where   you are

–think you've landed in
blank-time heaven

     – where it's 5 to 5 at

     25 past 11 . . .

MICHAEL HOROVITZ

. . . Where O where will wildness go
Now the sunshine turns to snow

The cold winds blow my spirits low
– The high winds call my spirit back

To flow and run – and ebb, for lack
Of clear direction. Alone I walk

Through empty streets, I talk
To no-one – none else abroad

– My pumping heart awaits the hoard
Must needs reward me at the next hilltop

But mounted to the crest I stop
Aghast – no promised land in harvest there

Instead a maze of prostrate trees, picked bare
– Derelict dwellings   – Where went the crop?

– A labyrinth of ruined fields that tear
My hope out

                    – Unidentified am I
– A last seed blown nowhere by the wintry sky

CROCODILES

Like squeaky toys, their noise
Makes children coo. Their little eyes
Like balls of wide surprise,
Are bugged for mother with
Her mouth of nails. And she,
With limbs like trees
And skin of knotted bark,
And weighing all a ton,
Collects her little ones.
Pouch-rocked in her throat,
She sets them free again
In water, with a tongue
As gentle as fingers.

LANDMINES

The legs are waiting.
There must be places in Heaven
Where they are stacked fifteen deep,
Along with fingers and arms
From industrial accidents,
All waiting for their bodies to die
and come to find them.

I may meet up with with
My womb again,
And a foot of colon that was severed
At its two ends
To become a worm in an Elysian field.

But every day I walk forward
I do not have to know
My legs have gone ahead.

MY FACE

As I sleep, other people
Wear my face. It is still
Worn out when I collect it
From the bathroom mirror
In the morning.

I haven't dared a surgeon yet,
To pick off the lines and
Cast adrift the boats
Of my eyes and nose
And mouth.

But in the forty years
That I have seen them all afloat,
Without a cord or chain
To anchor them between my ears,
Above my chin and throat,

My skin spiders and flesh-mites
Have been knitting up each
Facial twist and scratch. They even caught
The creases from my first laugh,
When I spilled out of the womb.

Longest worked on, it must
Run the deepest. A straight rope
From voice-box to navel. And if the line
Is taut enough, you will hear
It still plays the same note.

FRIEDA HUGHES

FRIEDA HUGHES

Scarred beneath their bags
Of heavy silicone,
They were mountains,
Shored up and sharpened,
A handful of the mind's mud
At a time. Those breasts

Weren't for a limp sweater,
Or a bra size more than
Two saucers. Those breasts
Had purpose. Men's eyes
Would unpage magazines
For a sight of them.

Melissa was no longer
Required to speak.
Her breasts could talk.
They had a language
And everyone
Understood.

When at last she made the photo shoot,
She gently placed her breasts
Of shiny plastic flesh
Upon the table for
The cameraman,
And left.

Is the elephant in the room.
We can't speak about it, even though
It stalks you. Thorny-haired,
Its eyes of nostril turning always to you,
As if you have some special smell.

It stalks us next, but for now
It wants you first.
You don't want its word
anywhere, or in our mouths.
Its presence makes us dumb.

So, it is the elephant in the room.
In my sleep, I take a gun
And shoot it dead. But in the morning
Its weight is at our feet again,
Wanting to be fed.

Its body is on the hearthrug
More faithful than any dog,
And beside the table, and
Beside you in the car, even though
I sit there; its mournful, stupid eyes

Unable to avoid you. Slowly,
Its breath is stealing your breath,
Its heavy feet rest upon
The altar of your chest. Tonight
I am going to kill it again.

FRIEDA HUGHES

OPPRESSION

at 12	when will I grow up
at 13	when will I grow up
at 14	when will I grow up
at 15	when will I grow up
at 16	when will I grow up
at 17	the wings beat and spread
	but my father appears
	yet again to cut me down
	for the seventeenth time.

BUSY BODY BEE

b z z z z z z
  b z z z z z z z z z z
    b z z z z z b z z z z

a busy body bee
fluttering in an onlooker's gaze
flies crossly past her placid sisters

b z z z z z z
  b z z z z z z z z z z
    b z z b z z z z z z z z z z z

in her home the woman quietly
goes about her work

b z z z z z z z z z z z z z z z z z

everything's straight
amongst honest whores

she turns

the visitor makes his moves
the play of their mirrors

she turns

clothes fall away
she turns

at dawn
she turns

no words   to be ashamed of.

NEVER AGAIN

It may have been fun while it lasted
The party look off like a jet
But now you feel pain-wracked and blasted
And full of the dregs of regret

When stars have lost their magic
And ditto the drugs and the men
Your soul reels soiled and tragic
Your brain cries "Never again!"

You try to reach the porcelain
Before you foul up your den
Last night's bad sights flash past you
You mutter "Never again . . ."

"Why me?" you whine
Until you recall
The awful behaviour
That led to your fall

All day you're feeling shattered
Till somebody calls you and then
Although your life's in tatters
You're ready to do it again

The action's all that matters
You're ready to do it again . . .

BEYOND A JOKE

We're at war
We can't make jokes any more
We should be partisan and reverent
Our old addictions are irrelevant

We're at war
We can't fool around like before
We should get seriously sore
And reinforce the wretched news
With scary vows and Gothic
views
We can't make jokes any more

Or can we?

I'm not really much of a singer
I try for a high note and croak
The critics may give me the finger
But fuck 'em if they can't take a joke

My act is obscene and offensive
I once made a publisher choke
They can't put me on the defensive
Fuck 'em if they can't take a joke

True to myself and toujours gay
That's how I am, that's how I'll stay
sometimes I fly sometimes I fall
But like they say – you can't win 'em all

My love life has been a fiasco
The last was a working-class bloke
I sprinkled his balls with tabasco
But fuck him if he can't take a joke

I've noticed that people are staring
My lyrics disgust decent folk
But my motto is always be daring
and fuck 'em if they can't take a joke

FRAN LANDESMAN

"O COME ALL YE FAITHFUL"

O come all ye faithful
Here is our cause:
All dreams are one dream,
All wars civil wars.

Lovers have never found
Agony strange;
We who hate change survive
Only through change.

Those who are sure of love
Do not complain.
For sure of love is sure
Love comes again.

Two from RED BIRD
(After Neruda)

#1

Lithe girl, brown girl,

the sun that makes apples
and stiffens the wheat
made your body with joy.

Your tongue like a red bird
dancing on ivory,
your lips with the smile of water.

Tantalise the sun, if you dare,
it will leave
shadows that match you, everywhere.

Lithe girl, brown girl,
nothing draws me towards you
and the heat within you
beats me home

like the sun at high noon.

Knowing these things,
perhaps through knowing these things,
I seek you out,

daft for the sound of your voice

or the brush of your arms against wheat,
or your step
among poppies grown under water.

#8

Tonight, I write sadly. Write
for example: Little grasshopper
shelter from the midnight frost
in the scarecrow's sleeve, advising myself.

The night wind throbs in the sky.

Tonight, I write so wearily. Write
for example: I wanted her
and at times it was me she wanted. Write,
the rain we watched last fall

has it fallen this year too?
She wanted me, and at times it was her
I wanted. Yet, it is gone, that want.
What's more, I do not care.

It is more terrible than my despair
at losing her. The night, always vast,
grows enormous without her, and
my comforter's tongue talking about her

is a red fox barred by ivory. Well,
does it matter I loved too weak to keep her?
The night ignores such trivial disputes.
She is not here. That's all.

Far off someone is singing.
And if to bring her back I look
and I run to the end of the road
and I shout, shout her name,
my voice comes back: the same, but weaker.

The night is the same night; it whitens
the same tree; casts the same shadows.
It is a dark, as long, as deep, and as endurable
as any other night. It is true: I don't want her,

but perhaps I want her . . .
Love's not as brief that I forget her,
so. Nevertheless, I shall forget her, and
alas, as if by accident

a day will pass in which
I shall not think about her even once.
And this the last line I shall write her.

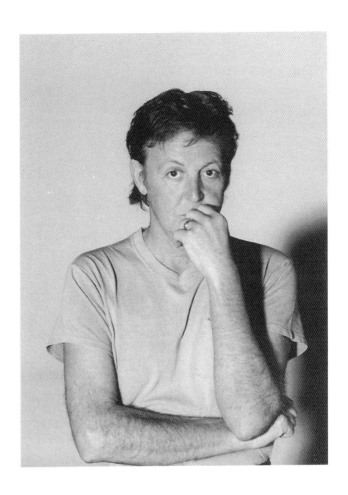

WHEN I'M SIXTY-FOUR

When I get older, losing my hair
    Many years from now,
Will you still be sending me a Valentine,
    Birthday greetings, bottle of wine?
If I've been out till quarter to three
    Would you lock the door?
Will you still need me, will you still feed me
    When I'm sixty-four?

    You'll be older too,
    And if you say the word –
    I could stay with you.

I could be handy, mending a fuse
    When your lights have gone.
You can knit a sweater by the fireside,
    Sunday mornings go for a ride.
Doing the garden, digging the weeds,
    Who could ask for more?
Will you still need me, will you still feed me
    When I'm sixty-four?

    Every summer we can rent a cottage in the Isle of Wight
    If it's not too dear;
    We shall scrimp and save.
    Grandchildren on your knee –
    Vera, Chuck and Dave.

Send me a postcard, drop me a line,
    Stating point of view,
Indicate precisely what you mean to say,
    Yours sincerely, wasting away.
Give me an answer, fill in a form,
    Mine for evermore.
Will you still need me, will you still feed me
    When I'm sixty-four?

Ah, look at all the lonely people.
Ah, look at all the lonely people.

EleanorRigby
Picks up the rice in the church where a wedding has been,
Lives in a dream.
Waits at the window,
Wearing the face that she keeps in a jar by the door,
Who is it for?

All the lonely people, where do they all come from?
All the lonely people, where do they all belong?

Father Mackenzie,
Writing the words of a sermon that no one will hear,
No one comes near.
Look at him working,
Darning his socks in the night when there's nobody there,
What does he care?

All the lonely people, where do they all come from?
All the lonely people, where do they all belong?

Eleanor Rigby
Died in the church and was buried along with her name.
Nobody came.
Father Mackenzie,
Wiping the dirt from his hands as he walks from the grave.
No one was saved.

All the lonely people, where do they all come from?
All the lonely people, where do they all belong?

Strings pluck, horns blow, drums beat.
Full-lunged songs sing enemies' defeat.
Sheep set loose, blacksmith's bench returned to use
and milkmaid's buckets spilled with glory tales.
Planted seeds found time to thrive
and farmers rose to reap their ripened wheat.
The warrior, at peace with peace
like thief, resolved to turn a leaf.
And lovers made lovers' plans.
Pebble games, daisy chains
and sub-chin butter tests.

Kids peel sticks of birch to feel
slick moistured fingertips.
Blue sky laced with tight white webs;
fields of high rye tickled skylarks,
levitating stars.

On contented drone of bee
musicians improvise a melody
fuelled by feast fermented fruit.
Sun-cooked air blew through flutes
and round bright maypole strings
a jig in plaited time thrilled quickened hearts.

Birds and butterflies flit
from wayside bush and ditch.
The track from town to stone
soon jammed with revellers
inching chattily towards
their sacred site
where she and he
vowed their proud love.
No kingdom could have crowned him
with more joy than her.

An impossibly distant black bird
circled overhead and wondered why
so many bite-sized creatures spent their lifetime
running on the spot.

"I was introduced to Tom Pickard by my late friend Allen Ginsberg. Tom helped me sort out *Standing Stone* –
a poem I wrote to accompany a piece of my music of the same name"

– from Paul McCartney's preface to Tom Pickard's fuckwind, *Etruscan Books 1999*

MEDITATE

Astride my inner peace
          I see
How many thoughts I throw
          at me

Stem this furious flow of frantic thought

     Meditate

Set aside arrangements to be made
Speeches to be spoken
Pennies on a plate

     Meditate

Listening to glistening bells
Ding dong mantras honey coat a parching thirst
Inner singer shouts out mantra
Down out lucy nation's chatter

Count for nothing
To count for count's sake
Count
To no total
To repeat
Not to remember, but
To not remember.

To meditate
To listen for nothing
Hear no reason

Mantra discovers
Naughty boy
Inside my mind
Trine to write poetry
Pa-boiled
Mam-marry

Gland opening

Ma shall law declare
Pa takes of the feast

Cunt hooks, quim, minge
Knob and tool
Words I often heard at school
Shall I fear to now repeat
Words that whistled down our street?

Stop

Man tra la la
Man trap

Stop

Mantra mantra

Love sound no meaning

Her spirit moves wind chimes
   When air is still
      And fills the rooms
         With fragrance of lily

Her eyes blue green
   Still seen
      Perfectly happy
         With nothing

Her spirit sets
   The water pipes a-humming
      Fat lektronic force be with ya sound

Her spirit talks to me
   Through animals
      Beautiful creature
         Lay with me

Bird that calls my name
   Insists that she is here
      And nothing
         Left to fear

Bright white squirrel
   Foot of tree
      Fixes me
         With innocent gaze

Her spirit talks to me

PAUL McCARTNEY

Blackbird singing in the dead of night
Take these broken wings and learn to fly
All your life
You were only waiting for this moment to arise.

Blackbird singing in the dead of night
Take these sunken eyes and learn to see
All your life
You were only waiting for this moment to be free

Blackbird fly
Into the light of a dark black night
Blackbird fly
Into the light of a dark black night

Blackbird singing in the dead of night
Take these broken wings and learn to fly
All your life
You were only waiting for this moment to arise.

PAUL McCARTNEY

HOT PURSUIT
(to Paul McCartney)

Augusta, Georgia,
Saturday night.
"Car Number Seven
Go break up a fight."

"Make it downtown
To the Franklin Hotel.
James Brown's in the lobby
And he's kicking up hell."

James Brown standing
Like a tall black tree.
"Hey little coppers
Did you come for me?"

"Hold it James Brown
Or we're gonna shoot."
But he took off in a truck,
Law in hot pursuit.

Cop car zooming
Right after James Brown.
He laugh like a jackass
Stuck his foot right down.

"Augusta, Georgia
Is my home town.
Shoot me if you dare
But I'm the famous James Brown."

"We don't care
If you're the great James Brown.
We'll shoot out your tyres
That'll slow you down."

Bam! One tyre
Got blown by their first.
Fired another bullet
A second tyre burst.

James Brown, James Brown,
They'll never catch him.
He kept on driving
On the metal rims.

"Catch me alive,
Or catch me dead.
Augusta, Georgia
There's sparkles round my head."

ADRIAN MITCHELL

"WE BOMB TONIGHT"
(headline in the Evening Standard, London, 17 December 1998)

"deafening explosions reverberated across Baghdad last night"

*"City traders reacted calmly to the air strikes, with oil prices
and the dollar retreating after yesterday's sharp gains . . ."*

me and little sister
sleeping tight
hugged in the arms
of a dark blue night

I was in a funny dream
and both of us
were being driven by a horse
in a dark blue bus

then my dream went bang
night turned day
little sister
was vanished away

and the air was nothing
but dust and screams
now I search for little sister
in all my dreams

she hides I seek
but all I have found
in my dreams is a
dark blue hole in the ground

Dreamed I was in a school playground i was about four feet high
Yes dreamed I was back in the playground and standing bout four feet
high
The playground was three miles long and the playground was five miles
wide

It was broken black tarmac with a high wire fence all around
Broken black dusty tarmac with a high fence running all around
And it had a special name to it, they called it the Killing Ground

Got a mother and a father they're a thousand miles away
The Rulers of the Killing Ground are coming out to play
Everyone thinking: who they going to play with today?

> You get it for being Jewish
> Get it for being black
> Get it for being chicken
> Get it for fighting back
> You get it for being big and fat
> Get it for being small
> O those who get it and get it and get it
> For any damn thing at all

Sometimes they take a beetle, tear off its six legs one by one
Beetle on its black back rocking in the lunchtime sun
But a beetle can't beg for mercy, a beetle's not half the fun

Heard a deep voice talking, it had that iceberg sound:
"It prepares them for Life" – but I have never found
Any place in my life that's worse than the Killing Ground.

ADRIAN MITCHELL

I remember God as an eccentric millionaire,
Locked in his workshop, beard a cloud of foggy-coloured hair,
Making the stones all different, each flower and disease,
Putting the Laps into Lapland, making China for the Chinese,
Laying down the Lake of Lucerne as smooth as blue-grey lino,
Wearily inventing the appendix and the rhino,
Making the fine fur for the mink, fine women for the fur,
Man's brain a gun, his heart a bomb, his conscience – a blur.

Christ I can see much better from here,
And Christ upon the Cross is clear.
Jesus is stretched like the skin of a kite
Over the Cross, he seems in flight
Sometimes. At times it seems more true
That he is meat nailed up alive and pain all through.
But it's hard to see Christ for priests. That happens when
A poet engenders generations of advertising men.

ADRIAN MITCHELL

NICE LUNCH

My Old Flame
Burns along the burnt siennas of the pub,
Chars the ham's pink and the cheese's yellow.

Memories in dust sheets
Hump together. And even if we could

Remember lunches when we couldn't eat a thing . . .
Nothing would be further away than your hand

Even later in the taxi's double bed.
The fangs of our denial are sunk too deep
For simple extraction.

WOMAN WAITING FOR THE TELEPHONE TO RING

This featureless statue has weathered centuries
But you can still distinguish
The pursing-forth of where the mouth was,
The unseeing sockets,
And the young incline of the neck,
Bared not for kisses
But the chop-chop of calculated silence.

Pine needles, each one an abyss
Like the dark place inside a guitar,
Browning the ground, aromatic, beneath me.
And the foam that spurted glassy and spectacular
And the most hidden crevices of rocks where a crab waited, one leg waving.
And first kisses, your whole body entrancing to you.
And Ambition, pitting your will against granite
Till a tunnel forms through which you wriggled, soiled but triumphant.
And travel, foreign spots smelling of inexhaustable beckonings,
And babies who make your body into your soul
(Their small heads as they bend over a task),
And the achievements of sinewy friendships, the lift of cavalier romance,
Even the touch of fabrics; the slow intention of a caterpillar;
Dully-acquired wisdoms; and – God – civilised attention to detail,
                    like spotting a ladybird's back.

       For all this I thank you.

But it's not worth it,
Not worth it
Not worth it
The hollowness inside without the lover
Who is always going going gone.
It isn't worth it,
To be a bell without a clapper
It isn't worth it,
Take it back
It's all wrong.

JILL NEVILLE

SPRING TIDE

(For Basil Bunting, Spring 1900 to Spring 1985)

1
A filthy winter to have lived through.
Dragged by the hair kicked and kicking into spring.

A year-long miners' strike,
broken.

Police road blocks blocked the motorways
and all roads leading to the north.

More reactionry than the thirties
the old fascist-fighting conchie told me.

2
While you lay dying in Hexham General Hospital,
we climbed Parliament Hill with our word learner son
to see the city from the lip of the basin
and to see the kites.

The little Geordie-Polak cried *keats*
when he saw the rainbow-winged mosquitoes
stringed against the cockney clouds.

You wanted sleep; a blood-clot
rushed to your brain. We pushed our faces into May:
snowflower our blossom told us,
thanking frothing hawthorn for the gift.

3
We stood by the North Sea,
a wash swirled around our feet.
Furthest from the shore
you stared towards a squall
on the dark horizon.

I warned against a threatening wave; swelling
it would overwhelm us.

Leaping to safety I glanced back and saw you,
steady, silent, still,
tracing the trajectory
of the wave's engulfing curve.

My son's warm hand on my leg
woke me drowning
in a cold sweat.

You, the dark spring tide,
and the spring
were gone.

DIANA AT HER BATH
(Rubens)

Diana,
her nipple
kissed pink
by the red dress
so recently removed
and rolling
the low light along
its narrow folds,
slips off
a white silk shift
and traps us
in the act
of seeing.

TOM PICKARD

QUIET PLACES

Some people on bus seats shake at the shoulders,
Stoned Elvises trying to dance after the gig

Some walk into the rain and look like they're smiling
Running mascara writes sad bitter letters on their faces

Some drive their cars into lay-bys or park edges
And cradle the steering-wheel looking like headless drivers

Some sink their open mouths into feather pillows
And tremble on the bed like beached dolphins

Some people are bent as question marks when they weep
And some are straight as italic exclamation marks

Some are soaking in emotional dew when they wake
Salt street maps etched into their faces

Some find rooms and fall to the floor as if praying to Allah. Noiseless
Faces contorted in that silent scream that seems like laughter

Why is there not a tissue-giver? A man who looks for tears
Who makes the finest silk tissues and offers them free?

It seems to me that around each corner beneath each stone
Are humans quietly looking for a place to cry on their own.

COLOUR BLIND

If you can see the sepia in the sun
Shades of grey in fading streets
The radiating bloodshot in a child's eye
The dark stains in her linen sheets
If you can see oil separate on water
The turquoise of leaves on trees
The reddened flush of your lover's cheeks
The violet peace of calmed seas

If you can see the bluest eye
The purple in the petals of the rose
The blue anger, the venom, of the volcano
The creeping orange of the lava flows
If you can see the red dust of the famished road
The white air tight strike of Nike's sign
If you can see the skin tone of a Lucian Freud
The colours of his frozen subject in mime

If you can see the white mist of the oasis
The red, white and blue that you defended
If you can see it all through the blackest pupil
The colours stretching, the rainbow suspended
If you can see the breached blue of the evening
And the caramel curls in the swirls of your tea
Why is it you say you are colour blind
When you see me?

LEMN SISSAY

ON THE LINE

Back in the summer of '84
We tried to help the miners win their war,
We came to do a gig for the GLC
That's Good Loud Country for you and me.
We came for music and now and then
For words of wisdom from old Red Ken
Who said "Three million people are unemployed
The heart of the nation is being destroyed"

No one knows you when you're on the line
They all want to help you when you're doing fine

There were hippies and punks and OAPs
UB40s and CIDs
But no one noticed them bad bad boys
With the bottles and the skins and the mouthful of noise
'Cos they slipped through the crowd like a shiver of fear
With them Air War steps that you never can hear.
And I knew what they were when I saw whem I saw them salute
And they knew I was a Commie from my flash pink suit

No one knows you when you're on the line
They all want to help you when you're doing fine

We started to polka and they went "Sieg Heil"
They jumped us and polka'd in our faces for a while
They knocked us down and put in the boot
Made a real mess of my flash pink suit.
They smashed a guitar, jagged like a knife,
And cut into the face of my friend for life,
'N there was no one to stop them, no security,
From the police, the crowd or the GLC.

END OF THE ROAD

I – I've had enough
Enough of the rain
Enough of the road
Enough of those wheels
Enough of the cold
And I want to go home
and I – I'm tired of the nights
The dazzling lights
When the wipers won't wipe
I can't see where I'm going
I can't know without knowing
And I'm headed on home
Hey hey please don't lock me away
On a steering wheel
I've got cowboy craziness burning inside
And I'm out of pills
Right now I could be warm
Lying in your arms
Healing your scars
So why am I here
With another flat beer
I want to go home.

ACKNOWLEDGEMENTS

Texts

Page 6: The italicised quotation is lines 23–30 of *The Waste Land* by T S Eliot (Faber and Faber, first published 1922);

7–8: Patience Agbabi's poems come from *Transformatrix* (Payback Press/Canongate Books, 2000);

12–15: Jean Binta Breeze's poems come from *Riddym Ravings & Other Poems* (Race Today Publications, 1988). You can hear Jean reading two of the poems on *Grandchildren of Albion Live*, the New Departures recordings *NDC23* and *NDCD24* (see top of page 80);

18–19: 'The Whole Mess . . . Almost' is in Gregory Corso's *Mindfield: New & Selected Poems* (Thunder's Mouth, NYC 1989/Paladin Books 1992) – but the text in this book restores some of the original version Corso contributed to *New Departures #12* (first Poetry Olympics Anthology, 1980);

20–21: 'Portland Coliseum' is in Allen Ginsberg's *Collected Poems* (Harper & Row and Viking Books, 1985);

28: Anselm Hollo's 'Pomology' was read by him at the First International Poetry Incarnation at Royal Albert Hall on 11 June 1965, and published in *Children of Albion* (ed M Horovitz, Penguin 1969);

30–32: Adam Horovitz's Orpheus and Eurydice poems are the first three in a sequence, originally written for the soundtrack to a fashion show entitled *Out of the Green*, which took place in Stroud, Gloucestershire in May 2001, as part of Stroud's Textile Festival;

33: ". . . this Eurydice made it . . ." first appeared in *The High Tower* (*New Departures #6*, 1970), and again in her posthumous *Collected Poems*, edited by Roger Garfitt (Bloodaxe Books and Enitharmon Press, 1985);

34–38: earlier versions of MH's 'Blank O'Clock Blues' appeared in the *'BIG HUGE' New Departures 1975,* and in *Growing Up: Selected Poems & Pictures 1951–1979* (Allison & Busby, 1979) – in which 'Reminder' and 'A Ghost of Summer' also appeared;

39–43: Frieda Hughes's poems come from *Stonepicker* (Bloodaxe Books, 2001);

46: Fran Landesman's 'Never Again' comes from *Stormy Emotions: New Lyrics* (Golden Handshake, 2001);

48–50: 'Two from *Red Bird*' and 'O come all ye faithful' are in Christopher Logue's *Selected Poems* (Faber and Faber, 1996). The two *Red Bird* texts are ". . . taken from a version of *Twenty Poems of Love and One of Despair* by Pablo Neruda (1904–1973) made by Patrick Bowles and me in 1954; revised by me in 1969"; all three poems are included on *Audiologue*, Christopher's seven-CD set of recordings from Unknown Public, 2001 – the Neruda versions with scintillating jazz accompaniment from the Tony Kinsey Quintet;

51–59: each of the Paul McCartney texts is in *Blackbird Singing: Poems and Lyrics 1965–1999*, edited by Adrian Mitchell (Faber and Faber 2001, © MPL Communications Ltd);

60–65: Adrian Mitchell's four poems come from *Greatest Hits* (Bloodaxe Books, 1991), *Blue Coffee: Poems 1985–1996* (Bloodaxe Books, 1996) and *All Shook Up: Poems 1997–2000* (Bloodaxe Books, 2000);

66–67: Jill Neville's poems first appeared in *New Departures #15*, 1983;

68–71: Tom Pickard's poems come from *Tiepin Eros* (Bloodaxe Books, 1994);

72–73: Lemn Sissay's poems come from *Morning Breaks in the Elevator* (Payback Press/Canongate Books, 1999);

74–75: Hank Wangford's songs can be heard on *Stormy Horizons*, his 1990 album with The Lost Cowboys (Sincere Sounds/New Routes).

Photographs

Front cover and Page 7: Patience Agbabi flying by Matt Livey;
6: US nuclear bomb test at Bikini Atoll, in the Marshall Islands, by Corbis. Many of Bikini's inhabitants evacuated after the first H-bomb tests there in 1946 were found to have ingested the largest dose of plutonium ever monitored in any population;
15: sunlight on the sea by A R Lomberg;
17: Claire Calman by John Alexander;
18: Gregory Corso with Edward Limonov and MH in September 1980 mapping out the first Poetry Olympics festival at Westminster Abbey, by Jane Bown;
21: Allen Ginsberg declaiming at the First International Poetry Incarnation at Royal Albert Hall, 11 June 1965, by Tom Picton;
28: Anselm Hollo by Graham Keen, early 1960s;
29: Adam Horovitz by Alfred Benjamin, late 1990s;
33: Frances Horovitz in the Cotswolds, by Bill Gardiner, 1976;
34: Michael Horovitz by David Trainer, 2000;
40: Frieda Hughes by Paul Massey;
47: Fran Landesman and John Hegley by Jackie de Stefano;
50: Christopher Logue at the POW! (Poetry Olympics Weekend) SuperJam at Royal Albert Hall, 6 July 1996, by David Evans;
51: Paul McCartney by Mary McCartney, 2000;
55: Tom Pickard and Allen Ginsberg by Linda McCartney, 1995;
58: Linda McCartney by Paul McCartney;
60: Adrian Mitchell at the Albert Hall POW! SuperJam of July 1996, by David Evans;
70: Basil Bunting and Tom Pickard at Warwick University in 1980, by Joanna Voit;
75: Hank Wangford by Trevor Leighton.

Illustrations

Page 26: *Orpheus Playing his Lyre* was painted by Duncan Grant (oils on paper, 15 inches diameter);
30: *Orpheus and Eurydice* was painted by Henry Fuseli (oil on canvas, 31cm x 39cm);
34: the picture-poem *Reminder* ("London's fair/ city spring . . .") was written and drawn by M Horovitz in 1962; it was first published in *Growing Up: Selected Poems* & *Pictures 1951–1979* (Allison & Busby, 1979);
37: drawing of birdy sax player off his ten feet by Michael Horovitz, late 1960s;
59: the blackbird was drawn by Paul McCartney;
63: *Gulf 3* is from Caroline Coon's 1992 series of watercolour prints touching on the brutal conduct and continuing reverberations of the Gulf War of 1991;
70: *Diana at her Bath* by Peter Paul Rubens can be viewed in the Borgmans Museum, Rotterdam.

ACKNOWLEDGEMENTS

(l to r) Alexander Trocchi, Anselm Hollo, Marcus Field, MH, Allen Ginsberg and John Esam on the steps of the Albert Memorial for a press conference on the day before the First International Poetry Incarnation at Royal Albert Hall on 11 June 1965, by Douglas Jefferey.

Adrian Mitchell and Paul McCartney backstage at the Southend leg of Paul's world tour in 1991, by Cyman Taylor.

Recent *New Departures* include the **POW!** and **POP!** Anthologies –
among others detailed overleaf, with photocopyable order form.

The POP! Anthology
A beautifully designed and printed Poetry Olympics
Party that brings together an unrepeatable company of
poets, writers, singer-songsmiths and musicians,
plus visual and performance artists for the pleasure
of your perusal

Includes –
John Agard
Patience Agbabi
Damon Albarn
Beryl Bainbridge
Samuel Beckett
Peter Blake
William Blake
Valerie Bloom
Jean Binta Breeze
William Burroughs
John Cooper Clarke
Carol Ann Duffy
Ian Dury
Harry Fainlight
Allen Ginsberg
Günter Grass
Thom Gunn
Seamus Heaney
John Hegley
David Hockney
Frances Horovitz
Frieda Hughes
Ted Hughes
Linton Kwesi Johnson
Jack Kerouac
Hanif Kureishi
R D Laing
Fran Landesman
Christopher Logue
Kirsty MacColl
Shirley Manson
Adrian Mitchell
Jill Neville
Moondog
Brian Patten
Kathleen Raine
Lamn Sissay
Stevie Smith
Stephen Spender
Joe Strummer
E J Thribb
Stan Tracey
Paul Weller

The POW! Anthology
An illustrated anthology of poets,
singer-songwriters, musicians and performance
artists of the world – to celebrate, commemorate
and consolidate the first Poetry Olympics
Weekend festival

Includes –
Damon Albarn
Simon Armitage
James Berry
Sujata Bhatt
Nina Cassian
Nick Cave
John Cooper Clarke
Ray Davies
Carol Ann Duffy
Paul Durcan
James Fenton
John Hegley
Miroslav Holub
Ted Hughes
Nerys Hughes
Jackie Kay
Brendan Kennelly
Hanif Kureishi
Mahmood Jamal
Christopher Logue
Roger McGough
Adrian Mitchell
Moondog
Grace Nichols
Ben Okri
William Shakespeare
Patti Smith
E J Thribb
Stan Tracey
Andrei Voznesensky
Heathcote Williams
Jah Wobble

ORDER FORM

CASSETTES, CDS, PUBLICATIONS AVAILABLE

Grandchildren of Albion Live on Cassette Volume One
—— (95 minutes) £8 each plus 75p p&p (incl VAT)* NDC 23, *ISBN 0-902689-15-0*

Grandchildren of Albion Live on CD Volume One
—— (78 minutes) £10.50 each plus £1 p&p (incl VAT)* NDCD 24, *ISBN 0-902689-16-9*
(Note: Ifigenija Simonovic's and Adam Horovitz's sets & Donal Carroll's 2nd/3rd poems omitted)

Grandchildren of Albion Anthology
—— (400-page illustrated) £9.99 plus £1.50 p&p* ND17-20, *ISBN 0-902689-14-2*
(Note: only sent for orders enclosing pre-payment in full, as very few copies remain)

Midsummer Morning Jog Log – 700-line rural rhapsody by M Horovitz
—— (Clothbound edition) illustrated by Peter Blake, £8.50 plus £1 p&p* *ISBN 0-9504606-7-2*

Michael Horovitz's Midsummer Morning Jog Log
—— (Paperback edition) illustrated by Peter Blake, £3.50 plus 75p p&p* *ISBN 0-9504606-8-0*

Wordsounds & Sightlines: New & Selected Poems by Michael Horovitz
—— (160-page, cover by David Hockney) £6.99 plus 75p p&p* ND31, *ISBN 0-902689-20-7*

The POW! Anthology, edited by Michael Horovitz and Inge Elsa Laird
—— (108-page illustrated) £6.99 plus £1 p&p* ND21–22, *ISBN 0-902689-17-7*

The POP! Anthology, edited by Michael Horovitz and Inge Elsa Laird
—— (128-page illustrated) £7.99 plus £1 p&p* ND25–26, *ISBN 0-902689-19-3*

The POM! Anthology, edited by Michael Horovitz
—— (80-page illustrated) £5.99 plus £1 p&p* ND32, *ISBN 0-902689-21-5*

Please photocopy this form, complete – entering number of copies required at left –
and send to: **New Departures, PO Box 9819, London W11 2GQ, United Kingdom**.

*If ordering outside the UK, please double the amount for postage and packing.

Allow 21 days for delivery (longer for outside the UK).

For more information about these titles and related publications/events,
visit our website ***www.connectotel.com/PoetryOlympics***
or write (enclosing a stamped addressed envelope if not placing an order).

I enclose a crossed cheque/postal order for £_____ made payable to **New Departures**
as total cost of this order including postage and packing.

Name

Address

Postcode